Albert Einstein
Gentle Genius

Don Herweck

Physical Science Readers: Albert Einstein: Gentle Genius

Publishing Credits

Editorial Director
Dona Herweck Rice

Creative Director
Lee Aucoin

Associate Editor
Joshua BishopRoby

Illustration Manager
Timothy J. Bradley

Editor-in-Chief
Sharon Coan, M.S.Ed.

Publisher
Rachelle Cracchiolo, M.S.Ed.

Science Contributor
Sally Ride Science

Science Consultants
Michael E. Kopecky,
   Science Department Chair,
   Chino Hills High School
Jane Weir, MPhys

Teacher Created Materials

5301 Oceanus Drive
Huntington Beach, CA 92649-1030
http://www.tcmpub.com
ISBN 978-0-7439-0572-5
© 2007 Teacher Created Materials
Made in China
Nordica.032015.CA21500127

Table of Contents

Albert Einstein may be the most famous **physicist** of all time. He is known both for his brilliant mind and his gentle spirit. He thought of things no one ever had. But he always stayed humble. He believed he was just one small part of the world, trying to figure things out.

Einstein was born in March of 1879 in Ulm, Germany. His family owned a business there. They made parts for machines. These parts helped the machines run on electricity.

Einstein didn't talk much when he was little. Some people thought he was not smart. He later proved this was far from true.

When Einstein was five years old and sick in bed, his father showed him a compass from the shop. Einstein realized that something made the needle move. That "something" was **magnetism**. He later said that moment was very important to him. It made him want to study science. He built models and mechanical things for fun.

Einstein, shown here with his sister Maja in about 1884, enjoyed physics-related puzzles even when he was a young boy.

He taught himself geometry by the age of 12. He was bored with regular school and often got into trouble there. He found ways to learn on his own. The family shop was a big help to his learning.

▲ A compass

▲ Einstein as a boy

Amazing Brain
After he died, Einstein's brain was studied. They found that it had an unusual shape. Some scientists think that the shape of his brain may have made him both slow when young and very smart at the same time.

Einstein's family moved often during his life. When he was one, they moved to Munich, Germany. Then, the family moved to Milan, Italy. Einstein was 15 at the time. He stayed behind in Germany for school. He wrote his first scientific work during this time away from his family. It was a paper on magnetism.

Einstein disliked his school very much. He loved to learn, but he didn't love his school's way of teaching. He finally left the school. He followed his family to Italy.

Einstein in the Bern patent office

Einstein's family wanted him to graduate. In 1896, they sent him to Switzerland to finish school. He trained to be a teacher of physics and math. When he couldn't find a teaching job, he took a job at the Swiss patent office. He became an assistant technical examiner. This meant that he had to review applications from inventors.

This clock tower in Bern existed in Einstein's time and still works today.

Important Scientist

Isaac Newton (1643–1727) was an English scientist, mathematician, and inventor. His three laws of motion are very important in physics. His work was key to the work that Einstein would later do.

Marriage and Family

Einstein married Mileva Maric in 1903. They had one daughter and two sons. Their marriage ended in 1919. In that year, he married his cousin, Elsa Löwenthal. She died in 1936.

▲ Portrait of Albert Einstein, 1947, about the same time that he began writing his most prominent theories

Einstein's specialty at the office was electromagnetic devices. He knew quite a bit about such things. He had learned a lot in his family's shop. This made his job easy. It gave him time to think about physics and the things he found important.

On his own time, he began to write science papers filled with new ideas. Once his ideas got out, the world would never be the same.

Einstein sent one of his papers to a university. They awarded him a doctoral degree. He sent another paper to another university. They made him a speaker at the school. He was made a professor of physics at a third university. By the age of 30, he was considered by many to be one of the world's leading scientific thinkers.

Einstein is known for solving a number of tough problems. Scientists of his time could not find the answers to these problems. They were using old ideas. They thought about things in old ways. Einstein found new ways to look at the problems. His new ideas changed the world.

Happy As Is
Einstein was known for being a bit of a slob. He didn't think formal dress was all that important. And he didn't like to wear socks. He said, "When I was young, I found out that the big toe always ends up making a hole in the sock. So, I stopped wearing socks."

Work That Changed the World

The year 1905 was a great one for Einstein. It was great for the world of science, too. He wrote four important papers. They became the building blocks for modern physics. It was also the year he earned his advanced degree.

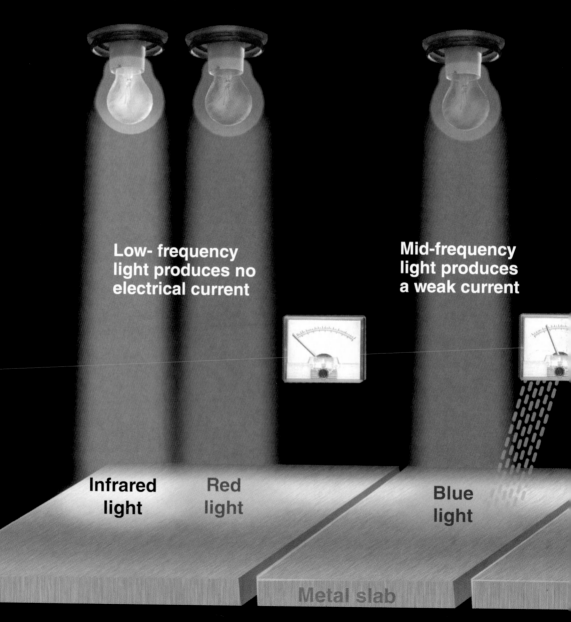

Low- frequency light produces no electrical current

Mid-frequency light produces a weak current

Infrared light

Red light

Blue light

Metal slab

Photoelectric Effect and Light Quanta

Einstein's first paper explained the **photoelectric effect**. Scientists had noticed something strange. They shined a bright light onto a metal surface. An electric current would run through the metal. They didn't know why this happened.

The paper started by explaining the work of other scientists. Einstein used math to describe the reasons for what they found. He explained why a small current flows through metal when light shines on it. He also explained that the current depends on color, and he told why this is.

Einstein experimented with colored light. He showed that blue light makes a current, while red does not. He also found that **ultraviolet light** makes a larger current than the blue light does.

What did it mean? Einstein wasn't finished.

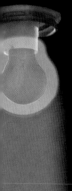

gh-frequency
ht produces
powerful
rrent

ltraviolet
light

Later, fellow scientist Max Planck would use Einstein's work on the photoelectric effect in his own work, for which he won the Nobel Prize. Planck managed to figure out the basic value of energy that one particle of light contains.

Einstein pointed out that different lights created different amounts of electrical **energy**. The amount of energy depended on the **light wave**.

Scientists knew that light traveled in waves. Red light has very low **frequency** waves. Blue light has higher frequency waves. Ultraviolet frequency is very high. The higher the frequency, the more energy the light wave has.

Einstein showed that the more energy is in the light wave, the more electricity it produces in the metal on which it shines. The light's energy was turned into electricity.

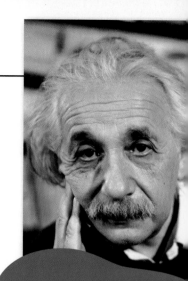

Einstein Said

"The most incomprehensibl thing about the universe is it's comprehensible." Einste meant it is amazing to know that the world's mysteries c be figured out.

Light quanta or photons

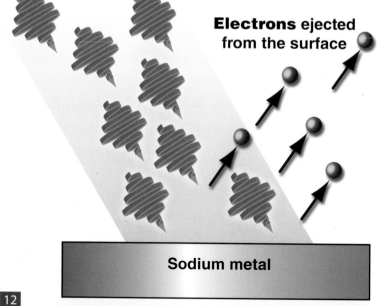

Electrons ejected from the surface

Sodium metal

Einstein's paper described **quanta**, or individual packets of energy. Light waves push these quanta around. Today, we call them photons. He explained that quanta cause the photoelectric effect.

Einstein won the Not Prize in physics in 1921 fc this work with light quan

Why Is the Sky Blue?

One example of light and color is right above us. It is in the sky and its blue color. Why is the sky blue? The answer is explained with light waves. Light waves are absorbed and scattered at different rates. Light with short wavelengths (such as blue) is scattered more than light with longer wavelengths (such as red). In the case of light from the sun, the blue waves are absorbed easily by dust, water, and other particles as light travels from the sun to Earth. As the blue light waves are absorbed, they are also scattered in different directions. So when you look into the sky, what you are really seeing are blue light waves scattered everywhere.

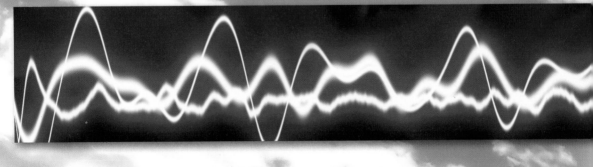

Brownian Motion

Einstein's second paper explained **Brownian motion**. In 1827, Robert Brown was studying pollen grains. He looked at them in water through a microscope. He noticed that the pollen grains moved around in the water. He didn't know why this happened.

Einstein explained this movement. The water drop was made of billions of water molecules. The reason the pollen grains move is due to the **molecules** (MOL-uh-kules) of the water hitting them. The pollen grain moves in random directions because the molecules hit from all different sides.

In this diagram of Brownian motion, the large green pollen grains are jostled about by the much smaller water molecules, which are always moving around.

In the Brownian assembly, the beach balls are jostled about by the students.

Brownian "Assembly"

To better understand random Brownian motion, think of a school assembly. Imagine everyone there. What would happen if all these people moved into a classroom? They would be tightly packed with little or no room. Now, imagine putting some huge beach balls in the room. They would stay in place because nothing in the room is in motion. So, what happens if everyone tried to move? The balls will be forced to move, although not very much. If everyone tries to run around the room, some of the people will be forced out the door. The balls will move faster and farther. The distance between people will increase. The temperature will even rise in the room. This is what happens with Brownian motion.

Special Theory of Relativity

The third paper of 1905 describes Einstein's **special theory of relativity** (rel-uh-TIV-uh-tee). It solved a problem with how people understood light.

At the time, scientists believed that light waves worked like waves in the ocean. Ocean waves travel through the water. They thought light waves had to travel through something, too. They called this substance *ether*. There was one problem. Two scientists made an experiment to measure the ether. They couldn't find any.

Einstein's paper started with the work of other scientists. He used their math to explain that light did not need to travel through anything. Light was different from ocean waves. Light always traveled at the same speed. That speed was a very big number. Instead of always writing the number, Einstein just wrote c.

▲ Albert Michelson

▲ Edward Morley

About Ether

Albert Michelson and Edward Morley weren't trying to disprove ether, but that's what they did. They made an experiment to measure how fast the ether carried light. They thought ether was moving. If they shined a light in the direction ether was going, the light should go faster. If they shined a light the other way, it would slow down. No matter which direction they shined the light, though, the speed was always the same. Ether wasn't carrying the light. It didn't exist.

Super Genius, Poor Speller

Einstein spoke and read both German and English fluently. But he was a terrible speller. He said he wasn't able to write English because he spelled so poorly.

Einstein wasn't done, though. Light was *very* different from ocean waves.

If you were on a sailing ship, you could travel along with the waves. From where you stood on the deck, the waves might look like they did not move. You could even travel faster than the waves. Then, the waves would look like they were going backwards!

Light works differently. Light always looks like it travels at c. Imagine you have a fast bicycle and your friend has a flashlight. Your friend shines the flashlight and you pedal in the same direction. No matter how fast you go, the light will still shine ahead as if you were standing still. How could that be? Einstein had the answer.

Einstein said that the faster you go, the slower time goes. At the same time, everything gets shorter. The front of your bike will shrink back toward the end of your bike. The more you try to catch the light, the slower time goes and the shorter you get. We don't notice this in everyday life. This only happens close to the speed of light.

Einstein showed that the old definitions of space and time had to be changed. They were two parts of the same thing, called *spacetime*. The faster you went, the weirder things got.

The girl is watching the bike rider travel near the speed of light. Notice that the bike rider's shape appears shortened.

While traveling near the speed of light, the world appears blurry to the bike rider.

Karen Magnus

Dr. Magnus is an American Indian. She is also a skilled scientist. She uses the high energy of X-rays to figure out the structure of a substance's atoms. She does this with crystals. When an X-ray hits a crystal, the X-ray diffracts. That means it breaks apart. This is like what happens when sunlight breaks apart to become a rainbow. The way that it diffracts tells about the structure of the atoms. Magnus says, "My scientific work has taught me . . . about flexibility, and the fact that you always have to be able to change your mind. For example, you may come up with a hypothesis, but your experiments may not show the results you expected. When this happens you have to be able to admit you were incorrect and move on!"

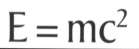

$E = mc^2$

Einstein's fourth paper in 1905 tells about the relationship between energy and **mass**. It says that the energy of a body (E) equals its mass (m) times the speed of light (c) squared. This is written $E = mc^2$.

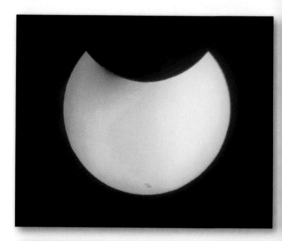

The equation shows that mass and energy are linked. It means that energy must behave the same as mass does. Not only were space and time the same thing. Mass and energy were the same thing, too!

This can be observed during a solar eclipse. A solar eclipse occurs when the moon comes between the sun and Earth, blocking the sun's bright light. During this time, we can see that starlight bends when it passes the sun. Light is energy that falls toward the sun, just as mass does.

▲ A solar eclipse in three stages

Jani Ingram

After Dr. Ingram earned her doctorate degree in 1990, she began working in a special lab. That lab was run by the U.S. Department of Energy. While there, she studied the waste that comes from making nuclear weapons. That waste is often harmful. It was her job to figure out what it does to the earth and how to clean it up. The work of Einstein and other scientists led to nuclear weapons used in war. Scientists like Ingram have been needed to figure out what happens next. They study how to clean up damage to the earth caused by the use of such weapons.

Ingram wants to make the world a better place through her work.

Einstein Said

"It followed from the Special Theory of Relativity that mass and energy are both but different manifestations of the same thing."

Love of Music

Einstein spent a lot of time thinking and studying alone. He needed a way to relax. Playing music on his violin became one of his favorite things to do. Some people said he wasn't very good at it. But he really enjoyed doing it.

General Theory of Relativity

There was only one problem with Special Relativity. It didn't explain gravity. The pull of gravity can be felt very far away. It also works instantly. The gravity of a star will pull you closer before you see its light. Did that mean that gravity moved faster than light? It took Einstein ten years to find the answer.

Einstein found that spacetime wasn't all the same. Some parts were bent and curved. The curves were easiest to see around large amounts of mass and energy, like stars. Planets and other small bodies could fall down the curves or roll around the edges. Gravity didn't travel faster than light. It wasn't a force at all. It was spacetime bending around mass and energy.

Einstein showed how gravity was actually the curve of spacetime caused by the mass of stars and planets.

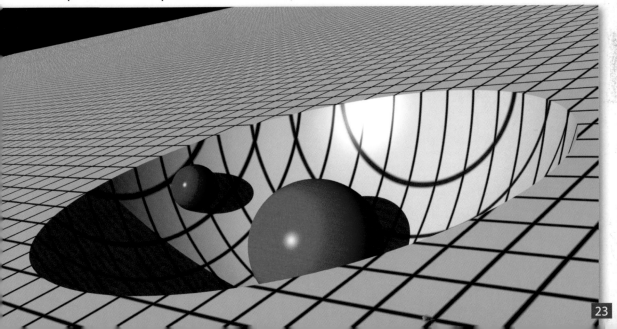

The Bomb

In the 1930s, Einstein was concerned about the German war effort. He was afraid the country would make and use an **atomic bomb**. Einstein didn't believe in war, but he did believe that action was needed. He wrote to President Franklin Roosevelt of the United States. He urged him to build the bomb before Germany did. This led to the Manhattan Project. It was a project in the United States to build an atomic bomb.

The project began in 1942. Einstein's work was very important to it. However, the bomb troubled Einstein. He didn't want it to be used. He knew that it would have terrible effects. In March of 1945, he wrote again to Roosevelt. Einstein warned him not to use the bomb. Roosevelt died in April. Einstein's letter was found unopened on his desk.

The next president, Harry Truman, did use the atomic bomb. He ordered two bombings of Japan in August of 1945. More than 200,000 people died as a result of the blasts. Japan surrendered soon thereafter. When Einstein

Einstein hoped that building the bomb would bring about peace. It was his wish that it would never have to be used.

heard the news, he dropped his head in his hands. He said, "I could burn my fingers that I wrote that first letter." He thought 200,000 deaths was too high a price to pay for the surrender.

Albert Einstein died on April 18, 1955, in Princeton, New Jersey. He left behind a wealth of work. It is still leading to new discoveries. With Einstein's help, scientists are learning more about the universe and its laws every day.

Taking a Stand
Einstein didn't like the things he saw happening in the country of his birth. He moved to the United States to become a professor of physics at Princeton. He then became a citizen of the United States in 1940.

Many people wonder what other scientific discoveries may have died with Einstein. He is pictured here at his 70th birthday party with his son and grandchildren.

Physicist: Persis Drell

Stanford Linear Accelerator Center (SLAC)

Persis Drell studies the smallest things in the world. They're teeny, tiny particles smaller than an atom. Drell works at a physics lab. At the lab, they shoot these particles down a tunnel that is two miles long. They go much faster than a speeding bullet. Physicists watch what happens when they hit a target at the end. Kaboom! Sometimes strange new particles are made. "I love figuring out what the world is made of at its most basic level," she says.

Drell also studies small things in space. Her latest project is a satellite built to collect particles coming from outer space. "I've never done anything like that before," she says. "But what I enjoy the most is when I don't know what I'm doing and have to figure it out."

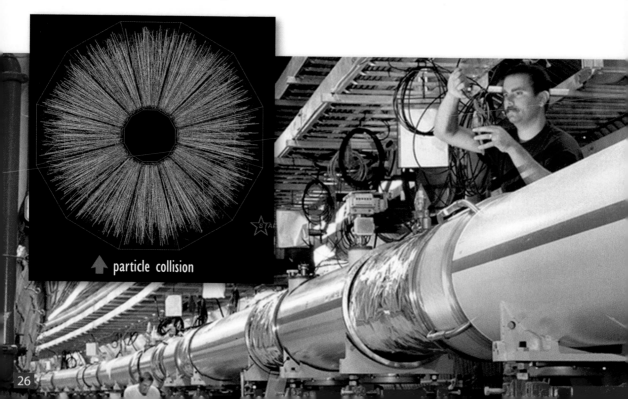

particle collision

Did U Know?

Most of the stuff in the universe is invisible. "We and everything that we are familiar with make up only 4% of the universe," Drell tells us.

Think About It

Drell did not like science as a kid. She even hated physics in high school. But in college she had great teachers who changed her mind. Who is your favorite teacher? Why?

Experts Tell Us ...

Drell says it is important to study math when you're young. "That's the language of science."

◀ Particle accelerator used to speed up particles

⬆ The GLAST satellite carries machinery that Drell helped develop.

Energy is the ability of a system to do work. It is power, and it comes in many forms. This lab experiment uses solar energy. Sunlight is solar energy. It is changed to heat when it is absorbed. It can be used to heat things. This experiment puts solar energy to work.

Materials

- cardboard box
- aluminum foil
- graham crackers
- chocolate bar
- marshmallows
- sun (solar energy)

Procedure

1   Cut the four side corners of the box nearly to the bottom.

2   Cover the inside of the cardboard box with the aluminum foil. Every side, including the inside of the top, should be covered. The shiny side of the foil should face out. This is a solar oven.

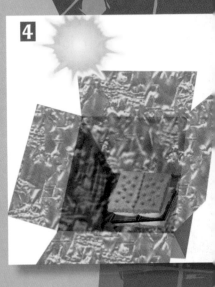

3   Make a s'more by putting some of the chocolate bar and marshmallows between two graham crackers.

4   Put the s'more inside the solar oven. Be sure to close the lid of the oven.

5   Place the solar oven in direct sunlight.

6   Check the s'more every 15 minutes. How long does it take for the s'more to cook? (The chocolate and marshmallow should melt.) What do you observe at each interval?

7   What does the cooked s'more say about solar energy? How did energy make the food melt? Try the experiment again with other foods such as bread and butter or bread and cheese. How do they behave differently than the chocolate and marshmallow? How are they the same? What do you think makes the differences?

Glossary

atomic bomb—a bomb created by breaking apart an atom, exerting devastating force

Brownian motion—a theory that explains how small particles like molecules move

electron–a particle that has a negative charge of electricity and travels around the nucleus of an atom

energy—the power to do work

frequency—the number of times something occurs within a period of time

general theory of relativity—Einstein's theory that explains the effect of gravity on the shape of space and the flow of time

light wave—visible electromagnetic radiation; the transfer of energy by regular vibration

magnetism—a natural force that creates attraction

mass—the physical amount of a solid body; bulk or volume

molecules—the smallest part of a compound that still retains the compound's properties

photoelectric effect—the giving off of free electrons from a metal surface when light strikes it

physicist—a specialist in physics, the science of force and motion

quanta—particles of an atom, now called photons

special theory of relativity—Einstein's theory that explains the motion of particles near the speed of light

ultraviolet light—located beyond the visible spectrum at its violet end and having a wavelength shorter than that of visible light but longer than those of X-rays

Index

Sally Ride Science

Sally Ride Science™ is an innovative content company dedicated to fueling young people's interests in science. Our publications and programs provide opportunities for students and teachers to explore the captivating world of science—from astrobiology to zoology. We bring science to life and show young people that science is creative, collaborative, fascinating, and fun.

Image Credits

Albert Einstein
Gentle Genius

Albert Einstein may be the most influential scientist and greatest physicist of the twentieth century. He revolutionized our ideas about time and space. He is best known for his theory of relativity and the equation $E=mc^2$, which explains the relationship between energy and mass. By age 30, Einstein was considered by many to be one of the world's greatest scientific thinkers of all time.

Physical Science

ISBN 978-0-7439-0572-5

TCM 10572